TEN THOUSAND MILES

BETWEEN US

TEN THOUSAND MILES

BETWEEN US

Rocco de Giacomo

To Matthew,

QUATTRO BOOKS

Thanks for a taste
of America's best
bacon.

Some of these poems, or variations thereof, have appeared in the following publications: *Arc Poetry Magazine, Contemporary Verse2, Tower Poetry Society, Prairie Journal, Birmingham Poetry Review, White Wall Review, Textshop,* and *Cha: An Asian Literary Journal.* Some have also appeared in the chapbook collections *Latchkey Soul* (Sirens Press, 2000), *Hostel Lives* (Sirens Press, 2000), *Leaning into the Mountain* (Fooliar Press, 2006), and *Catching Dawn's Breath* (LyricalMyrical Press, 2008).

 Canada Council for the Arts **Conseil des Arts du Canada**

We acknowledge the support of the Canada Council for the Arts which last year invested $20.1 million in writing and publishing throughout Canada.

Cover photograph: Rocco de Giacomo
Author's photograph: Lisa Keophila
Cover design: Diane Mascherin

Library and Archives Canada Cataloguing in Publication

De Giacomo, Rocco
  Ten thousand miles between us / Rocco de Giacomo.

Poems.
ISBN 978-0-9810186-7-6

I. Title.

PS8557.E3684T46 2009   C811'.6   C2009-904597-4

Published by Quattro Books
P.O. Box 53031, Royal Orchard Postal Station
10 Royal Orchard Blvd., Thornhill, ON L3T 3C0
www.quattrobooks.ca

Printed in Canada

TO VITO

Contents

I.

II.

I.

BEGIN

This starts
when I am 12 years old:
my cousin and I
are clearing his back yard of trees
and forcing the branches and bits
of fresh
wood into the mouth
of a little red shredder
he's just bought in town.

We've been at it all afternoon
feeding this machine
and watching the chips fly
when my left hand
gets caught
in a tangle of branches,
pulling my arm towards the mouth
of the shredder

I've been screaming

fingers
hand
arm

                                             cheek
grass
                              brick
          breast
                    window

minutes
                         skin

the holy unwant
bits of me
fly clean
from the spinning teeth of a
back
yard
sun
turning
in the mouth of
every word
I'll ever write.

At the last second
my hand slips free.

Be careful with that
my cousin says
stuffing more wood
into the machine.

TO THE OLD

Your voice
is a mahogany balustrade
we follow
with a museum kindness
an obligatory wonder
into collections
suffocated
behind glass.

You were like us once,
fearful
tender
the world was a closet
looming with detail;
you were fleeting
as perilous as shadows under blades of grass,
slipping lightly
between teeth,
feeling for the coolness
of sun-breaks
and half heard secrets,
promising
we could all taste
like lake water and feel
like wind-dried cotton.

But now, even your fury
is polished, every
word a marble face.
This is your shelter,
your varnished rage.

The youngest of us
snicker, the oldest smile
and pray
that one day soon
your tongue will cleave,
your archways collapse,
and we will speak through
into a deeper zodiac
whose stars are now
crackling in your blood.

NOSTALGIA

My mother
touches my shoulder,
points, and says: *look up,
you can tell if it's a hawk
by the curl in its wings.*

I am being carried
with slow drifting sight
from the ends
of her voice
into the sun,

and
after 10 years
of travelling
the height of dreams
along the span of day and night
I recede from a backseat window
finding myself
curled in her words
as I move through
open fields.

AS YOU FALL ASLEEP

I am on the brink of you,
a boy
captivated by the expressions
      falling from under you
watching the depths bloom
              beneath your skin,
so badly wanting to reach in
and become
a whim of what you are
in there:
a figment of a breeze,
a ghost kiss, perhaps
but so very scared
of how far I might fall.

LIGHTNING

If this was happening when we first met
you would have glanced out at the splintering
volts, hotter than noon suns firing randomly
over the startled trees into the cavernous
theatre above our tent, and would have said
this was nothing but God moving his furniture
and taking cute snapshots with the flash
to show his friends. If this was then, you would
have even tried to go back to sleep.
But we're married now, and when I shake
you awake you rub your eyes as if
readying them to see the world as I do:
a procession of gruesome deaths, narrowly
missed; a macabre parade of ghastly
possibilities whispering strange poems
as it passes. In your eyes,
                              turbulence
at cruising altitude may very well be
bumps in a country road, but the thought
of an atheistic aviophobe plummeting
30,000 feet while screaming *Hail Mary
full of grace* makes much better poetry.
And it is only when we are halfway between
the tent and car (me in hiking boots
and white briefs, you in winter leotards
and knee-high black wellies, both of us
looking like Noah's in-laws from the city,
shuffling under a tiny red umbrella) that I
realize my mistake, and think

How perfect is this! Are we!
Naturally, I say nothing
of it as you play out
the silent course of my fears,
asleep in minutes while I gauge the strength
of the sunroof and correct the grammar
in tomorrow's tragic headlines.

MICHELANGELO

Michelangelo got it right
when he snuck in one night
and chiselled his name
across the virgin's chest
to mark her as his own.

And he got it right when
he made David out of stone
with the lips of a poet,
the chest of a bully, the shoulders
of a slave and the hands of a killer;
a simple assortment of abilities
to get us from here to there.

With Samson it was about
swinging a jawbone,
with Martin Luther King Jr.
it was about uncurling a fist,
with Mahatma Gandhi
it was about not moving
at all, and with me for now
it's about lying here with you.

And you will whisper *yes*
and nod your head into my neck.
I am as still as stone
as you shudder slightly into sleep,
your one fingernail secretly
trying to chisel your name
across my chest.

OUR BODIES LIE BY THE WINDOW

the sky is purple
and pink where
the wakefulness touches;
your legs and stomach
are gold and white,
our eyelids
flicker against
the stillness
of movements that
almost make me
want to
notice things,
how they
draw in the noise
outside us:
the rails of an electric bus
circling the cobwebs on the ceiling,
airbrakes nudging our breaths in
and out to where
two junkies sit
on the curb,
their whispers
brushing our curtains;
across the street
the lights are
blinking,
struggling as they sink
into dawn.
They grasp at us,
capture us

as living gestures
while we close our eyes
and hold this room
by a thread
and let the stars drown
all the rest
with light.

SUCKER

When Joseph heard the news that God had chosen Mary
he might have stood in his little shack
a little stunned, a little surprised
by the turn of events in his marriage.
And watching Mary hum about, happily packing her bags
while Gabriel waited at the door, he might have looked down
at the silly gift he had bought her
and asked, *what did I do?*
And she might have answered:
Don't make me choose.

And we are told men should know this already:
that a woman's preference for the divine
should be an easy circumstance to accept.

Should it?
Imagine for a second:
What if he was a she?
What if God was a Goddess?

Do you think Mary would have looked so placid and brilliant
watching Joseph leave for a little rendezvous
with the One above?
Or would the ivory-fresco calm of her face darken
just a little from jealousy?

And you,
would you have been so damned tenacious every Sunday
    morning
to pull me out of bed
tired and grumpy

just to watch me bow my head and surrender
to some loving prophetess?

No,
you would have coiled your slender limbs around me and said:

Stay
be with me
don't go to her
I'm real
I'm flesh and blood
I'm bruised but sweet
battered and beautiful
I can be your slave
I can be your Goddess
don't pray to her
pray to me.

And under our sky of summer sheets
I would have closed my eyes to paradise and remained.

So, locked out on your porch
I was a little stunned, a little surprised
by the turn of events in our relationship
because when Gabriel called for you,
you did not remain.

I guess God has made you able to see
beyond the shacks and summer sheets
to his castle in the sky, and he has made me
too proud to beg and too scared to mess
with the loaded dice, rolled against whatever loyalty

I have left.

I peek through your curtains,
now, hear your worship
and I wait, like a sucker
for you to come back down.

IMMINENCE

We put away our dishes
and left the campsite
for a walk. You finished
crying and the night hung
above us like a secret
broken among lanterns.

We couldn't tell where
the cosmos ended
and the lights from
the Winnebagos began.
But there they were,
great mammoths
horoscoped into the stars,
old wedding rings
and eyeglasses dying
in their orbits under
the midnight shade
of leaves.

It's amazing what
the world becomes
when you are wounded.
The rattle of dice, an
asteroid belt, the cherry
of a cigarette, a collapsing
star and the distant laughter
of a woman. The beginning
and ending of all things.

RE: FOUND SOMETHING

Now,
I know
we are old coats to each other:
out of style,
torn at the seams,
laughable
and honest
with the efforts
to put each other away.

But it rains here
and it's cold
and trying you on
the other day
I found this
in one of the inside pockets:

Having driven through the snow to Niagara Falls,
we are sitting inside a coffee shop, listening
to each other speak and drink and breathe,
watching the world outside quietly layer itself
in mist and ice and snow. And the sun breaks
from the clouds for a moment, and the reaches
of the Peace Bridge turn gold over your shoulder.

Now,
I know
it's only a moment
and I know
we have long since shed each other

for newer things,
but sometimes
when it's raining
and cold

I need to dig deep,
slip inside
these old fabrics
to keep myself warm.

WAKING

6:00 AM is the long stretch
of visions and oddities rubbing their eyes,
pulling over wherever they are, and letting
the minutes pass. A dining table is found
standing on a landing strip, a new species
of laughter lies down in your closet; there,
out of time's way, these dialects, like shadows
of trees, rise and fall on eyelids and eardrums.
The pounding of floorboards, the steady breath
of traffic mean something else now: a fading
unfamiliar serenade, near voiceless;
a withered hand, full of grace.

Curl these fingers
into beach sand and bed sheet:
this last hour is a blessing, mixed.

PERFECT

a ripe tomato
fat enough
to burst
an afternoon
ringing with rain
and laughter
bright and beading
with tears
sweet enough
to shatter with a fist
thrown out of love
and then you
lying there
gleaming
slipping through things,
light bleeding
through a rose,
you can't
for the life of you
you can't
believe
the way green stalks
of long grass feel
against your neck
you can't
believe
the raisin smell of boat gas
the clear deafness of a lake
can't believe
the creak

of an old ladder
the fullness of a berry
between fingers
believe
the weight of thunder
the slap of lightning
or
whatever
finally
broke us
the wind
blazing
the moon
dying
and you
lying there
breathless
seeping joy,
blood moving
through a bruise,
the mistakes scattering
in the laughter of glass
made perfect
against a cherry tree
awash in the storm

MY LITTLE ANVIL

I'm glad to see you here
because I went to bed angry last night
and I heard the blacksmith
knocking about,
I felt his blind eyes
burning my insides
for fuel,
I tasted his fingertips
as he choked
my dreams
for ink and anything
tangible enough
to hammer out.

And seeing you here
truthed in arcs
of blank on white
I realize
that in my sleep
I let you go
just in time
before I
pulled you across my little anvil
and pounded you
into these words.

MEN LIKE US

We'll be here when all this shudders, a fist
against plate glass;
when all this bursts, a bomb
into the stillness
of forests and stolen kisses
tucked neat
and clean
in these palms,
playing cards dealt
with the rough mistrust
of old fingers.

We'll be here
at these tables
these ashtrays
these booths, these caves
deeper than hope
thoughts deadlier than cigarettes
lingering halos
beyond the reach of our words
where TV screens can glow round
in the distance of heroes
or close and cryptic
with the shoulders
and faces of a riot
going on in some inner city.

The screens
slither with light,
cracks in the door of a distant hell,

except it's not hell
it's an isolated truck stop
or a twenty-four-hour coffee shop
or a late night pizza parlour
that just happened to have seats where
men like us
can come and sit
and let fingers fumble a cigarette,
let lips drain a glass;
dreams and memories mix
like sugar and water,
so the missed buses
the lost money
and the dreams never realized
become mermaids on rocks
or foul balls into bandstands:
things worth
a lifetime of waiting
but far too beautiful to have.

We'll be here
patient as priests, our moon skins
drawing up the sins
from shadows across the floor,
our ivory faces
glowing in the heat of
this being
burning blindly
until we shudder and burst
into quieter apocalypses
where bottles break
and fists slam

and TVs and worlds
burn and burn,

collapse while
we are all
taken down by dogs.

And then
years from now
there we are
over your shoulder
cane in hand
in the light of an open doorway
in the middle of a city street
slicked with rain
in the shade of a willow tree
on the bank of some blue bay,
palms empty as parking lots
smiles full as if knowing
that we've always been here,
that this life
has well been worth the while.

Until then
we'll be here
where the waitresses
carry the gentle urgency of
night nurses
being told
to give us our drinks
and empty our ashtrays
lest a neglected glass
or burnt knuckle

or a dream gone unrecognized
ignite a riot
out of the brittle calm
of all this waiting.

EARLY BIRD SPECIAL

Lately, Jesus has been wearing a white fedora
because he hopes it will help his friends spot him
in crowded restaurants. He looks around, then at his watch,
sighs, and returns to dipping his toast in the bacon grease.
Jesus doesn't understand it. He calls, they *say yes my lord,*
Sunday, 8:00 AM, I'll be there and then nothing,
not even a voicemail explaining why they've stood him up.
The waitress is putting another old guy with him at the table.
What? Is this a playdate now? He's not going to say a thing
to this guy. The other feller gives him one of those toothy
dentured smiles, but Jesus pretends not to see it,
looks instead in the mirror along the wall.
The white Fedora is too big for his head.
He's getting on in years, he knows that, but *is his skull*
shrinking? The hat isn't so much sitting on his head
as he is sitting under it. Is this what happens?
Height, hair, bowels and joints, and now skull size?
Everything's going. All that's left are these Sundays
in Moose Jaw, quiet hours to wiggle a razor
under his chin, fiddle with a Windsor knot, and wait
for a friend to show up. Well, end of the line, rock bottom,

he swallowed his pride and phoned number thirteen,
and now even the bacon grease is cold. Thinking about it,
though a little crestfallen, he's not that surprised.
None of the other guys trusted him; but Jesus,
Jesus had liked him, kinda; pretty much the same way
Wally or Winky or whatever-the-heck his name was
liked Eddie Haskell. You couldn't leave your wallet
around the guy but on those hot days when the others

were wailing and ranting in all that fevered purity,
Jesus found the cool deviousness of this one refreshing.
It would have been nice to see him again. That whole business,
in that garden? What's the name again? Gethsemane!
Water under the bridge. In fact, Jesus had prepared a joke
about hitting him up for the proceeds on that deal,
maybe using them to pay for the bacon and eggs, *Ha ha.*
Something deep and twisted using that money to pay for bacon.
Ah, well, Jesus thinks to himself as he fishes for his wallet,
maybe it's not that funny. Too soon, too soon. He pulls out a tenner,
then he thinks: *Well, why break precedence?* So he fishes deeper,
and on the way out he whispers to the cashier, letting her know
that he's paid the tab again, for everyone.

WHY TAKE THIS PICTURE?

try
to imagine
the angle
with which you
could catch me

try
to imagine
the wind about my arms
twirling
colours frozen
in the silence of
just another
black and white

try
to imagine
me
young and svelte
a stray note dangling
on the ends of songs
you can almost
recognize

try
to imagine gravity
and concrete
and sinew
and bone

try
to imagine
the light of windows behind me
staring like children
who never learn
that beauty fades
and holds only
for a moment
these words
as I dance coral
oblivious as
someone
who hasn't realized
they've forgotten
their lines

try
to imagine
yourself
up against all this
with only a
lens
and a finger bent
while the brownstones hold back the light
and the streetlamps string their syllables
into a single gaze
and now
do anything
but take this picture

HANDS

I am curled on a bench.
My hair is a mess, eyeglasses cling
to my face as I sleep palm to palm
under a tree in a Chinese shopping mall.

You would never tell me why
you took this photo; another life
and now you wonder how
the picture could have fallen
from the shelf, my dreams frozen
there as graceless as any man's
prayers. You restore the picture
and recall how you placed my shoes
tidily at the foot of the bench; the way
I simply scrunched my jacket
into a pillow after you got up.

I always forgot to button down
my collar, and you remember
the many mornings you helped me
with my tie, your fingers working
methodically in the stillness,
always close enough to hear
the sound of passing cars. Even now,
other men fall helplessly asleep
on the shaded benches in the Fragrant Hills,
or haphazardly on mats along Sanlitur.
Each of them a little accident wishing
to find itself rescued by smaller,
purposeful hands.

OLD HOUSES

In old houses
the attic door opens
on the bottom of the sea.
Lifting the heavy lid
you peek into the dark
from under a stone.

A leather harness
for a prosthetic arm
floating in the pale debris,
a discharged shotgun shell,
the silver nameplate of a grave marker,
the dried corpse of a squirrel:

All this intrigue
gone uninterrupted
for years, while fathoms below
you dreamt only of autumn days
smouldering through dark cracks
of wood.

HEY, HAS ANYONE SEEN...?

The place should be vacant,
but the man is on his feet as I enter
the upstairs room, shirtless, barefoot,
needle-thin. *Hey folks,* he says, *this is my room,*
and he brings his bony hands together with a brittle
clap. He is already the vision
of how he wants to be
remembered. *Sorry for the mess,*
but what can you do?

I'm asked if I'd like to see more,
another room, maybe? I decline.
He smiles, nods at me. I return the gesture,
and so does the real estate agent. We all smile
and nod our way back down the stairs,
and I begin to wonder how we even got to be
on the second floor
of an abandoned house
in a bad neighbourhood
in the first place.

But this is how you vanish;
horror movies are all true:
every time, despite all the warnings:
in through the weathered Polaroid
past the stained mattresses and dead
houseflies and up the creaky staircase,
all while your car seat is still warm
and the coffee rings have yet to dry
on your kitchen table.

Near the end, you'll hear what you think
is TV static in an empty room
or the sound your ears make
in the deepest part of the pool,
but what you never realize in time
is that this sound
has always been
that of a distant audience
crying out: *Don't go there,*
don't go in there.

NEW HOUSE

My new house is empty, the wind
cuts through the cracked windows,
I push my fingers against the frigid
glass, remember walking behind
my father, stumbling in the footprints
he made in the snow as we hammered
sheets of plastic to the windows
of our old farmhouse.

Inside we walked among the vacant
rooms; they were silent, sealed
and draining to cold like a thought,
a motion, a gentle gesture held tight,
squeezed to warmth and left
in the snow.

It's been years and thousands of miles
and the farmhouse is gone – rubble
under ice – but the rooms are here.
When we talk on the phone
we stumble through high drifts,
our words leave no footprints,
our silences give no direction,
and breathless between each other
we feel for cracks and openings
we might have overlooked, ways
into spaces once warm, to the doors
and windows we shut and sealed tight
a long time ago.

THIRTYSOMETHING
To Jacob

I now refer to teenagers as punks,
modern music as *all the same garbage,*
and twentysomethings as *romantically masochistic.*
Lately, Jacob, trying on second-hand jeans at Courage My Love
feels like sitting on a warm toilet seat in a public bathroom.
I don't know why, but it's probably the reason my house
reeks of Ikea now: a mixture of pine, polyurethane and
sugared guilt; Afghans sewn by Swedish virgins
and bookshelves the colour of affluent wooden dentures,
appropriated from the wealthy mouths of our forefathers,
proudly displaying my dusty dog-eared socio-political-historical
dissertations, and a dark, growing mass of pulp horror. This is not
a dumbing down, Jacob, it's just that when I've spent the day
swinging from a ladder, wishing death upon the squirrels
digging under my eaves trough, Stephen King speaks to me
in a way that Jacques Derrida, Noam Chomsky or
Jared Diamond can't. The people at Home Depot run
when they see me, Jacob; my sponsored child,
finger in her nose, peers at me from her dirt village
in Kenya. The coffee from her country tastes like spiced earth,
and yes, I am aware of this awful arrangement, just as I am aware
of the sunflower heads that I keep kept in tap water
and how they droop over the mouth of the Chinese fertility vase
like tragic streetlamps: they're beautiful, Jacob,
and I'm beginning to need comfort now and then, the
occasional taste of bliss. I could never understand
my father's fascination with *Hee-Haw,* nor my mother's
obsession with gaudy ornaments, but when I was 24

I went to a communist cell meeting at Ossington and Bloor
to find no garbanzos, no angels or sentiment, just a Spanish
cross-dresser railing against his parents. There should have been
a manual for being a thirtysomething, Jacob, much like the Sex Ed
handouts we got in grade six, but with more unwanted hair and tips
on how to hide internet porn from your wife,
how to use a caulking gun without making a sticky mess,
and how to cope with the realisation that despite Billy Corgan's rage,
we're headed for tea cosies, Werthers Candies, and purses filled
with warm pennies. Jacob, I must tell you
that when I sat in a heated leather bucket seat last week I swear
I found heaven dawning along my spine.

II.

OVERNIGHT BUS

It's late,
very dark; the one beside you
is snoring and you don't know
exactly where you are.

Around you is a terrain con-
torted by sleep; the awkward,
heavy burden pulling at your tired
body, collapsing like a card table
under the weight of the shoulder
beside you, the knee or foot
in your back, the ring finger
and pinkie of your left hand
that are slowly falling asleep
without you.

A nostril whistles like an asthmatic
sparrow; a sweat-sock dangles
from a foot like a dried snakeskin.

In this country you witness everything
in stealth; you are a stowaway,
a cat burglar balancing your head
on a wallet-sized pillow
stealing warmth from a blanket
the size of a dishcloth: you are

a secret lover crouching
in a bedroom closet, defiant, proud,
at least until morning

when light oozes into your eyes
and all you can do is cover your face
with your arm, rise from where you were,
as from a pile of leaves, and climb
down the front steps, yesterday's pants
unwinding from your legs like rough
twine, the look on your face saying,
I don't usually do this.

HIGHWAY

The road is a line of wire,
each town is a little sound
we pluck, consume between
sneezes and coughs and words
we restlessly exchange.

It's the plump numbers
we long for, the ones
hanging from the bottom
of highway signs, waiting
like ripened bells.

RESTAURANT AND CAFÉ

Romance is where blue-haired ladies
nibble at egg salad sandwiches,
prairie skies hang from roofing nails,
and on the AM radio, the price
of canola is discussed as often as war.

It's where the contents of our
sandwiches are applied with
ice-cream scoops, the trays
are mint, the linoleum squeaks
and slices of pickle are an extra 50¢.

It's where spoonfuls of borscht
paint our mouths red, our legs stick
to the seats, and our lips
are like ribbon smears on a white canvas:
the words *I love you* a tongue's-breath
away from ruining and meaning everything.

CREATING SASKATOON

Brahms plays to an empty bus stop.
And the benches, the shelter,
the little trees along 22nd Avenue
keep very still, not wanting
to tell the loudspeaker that
it's a Sunday.

Three tightrope artists practice
in the park by the river. There is
something disappointing about this.
Grim-faced seraphim
at 80 feet, here they wobble
between tree trunks like sailors
at dawn.

Men are urinating
against the base of the Broadway
Bridge. This morning they are
captivating. For you, anyways
as you confess that you have never
before seen a urinating penis.
I confess that when I was young
I would yell *Jesus Christ
is my Saviour* out my
bedroom window. You then
point out the spirals of hair
on my forearms, and Brahms

plays to an empty street,
breaks upon red brick, and dissolves
into the lingering noise,
this repair shop for stars. Empty,
the world here is far less
than the sum of its parts.

As we pass, a young Goth
draws aside her long black lace,
shows us where the
moonlight is.

CAMPSITE 76

The tent wants to talk about your life:
What are you doing *here*, at your age?
But you lie so wilfully against
the unforgiving earth, that even the stars
want out of the discussion and stare blankly
ahead; the trees shuffle their leaves
nervously. The tent takes a breath,
then sighs, not quite sure how
it's going to bring this up.

RV PARK AND CAMPGROUND

Someone is burning garbage, the smoke comes
in acrid waves; Lisa holds her breath and applies
OFF! Spray as liberally as sun-block and I hold
my nose as I try to test the pasta sauce
in the simmering pot, balanced on the little
Coleman burner that rests on the little
propane canister at the very edge of the picnic table
that wobbles every time one of us swats a mosquito;
kids ogle us from Big-Wheels like orangutans at a circus,
chewing on Mr. Freezees the size of Cuban cigars,
sizing up our two-man tent, pitched on this gravel drive,
while two old men in office socks and sandals
fart and grumble on a wooden bench, and a 300-pound lady
with spindly legs sips at a can of Blue and scribbles
in her diary as proud as the 10-year-old shouting
to his Grandma from high up on a branch:
You can't find me! You can't find me!
Grandma smiles in her lawn chair and whispers
oaths as old as the trees that serve as a fence
between here, where fathers sing in the concrete
showers with their baby boys, and the golf course
next door, where adults in pastel blue drink
brandy from finger-sized bottles, tilting their heads
skywards as the colours drain like the last swallow
of Peach Schnapps at a Grade 8 dance: a place where
no one wants to be, but when all they've got
are homemade haircuts and lingering highs,
all they have is the recklessness to say:

What the fuck are *you* looking at?

BEAR COUNTRY

They haven't mentioned
that the soap, the toothpaste,
the spices carried away on winds
will turn you into a saviour.

Consider though, the terrain
of berries and rock, the ochre core
of bone over your wine-red muscle.

Consider the small pot of meat
and beans warming your face,
its rosy flesh, the iron deep
in your liver. Then stir the pot
and spill the honey, the parish
of birds will watch, silent
Eucharist bells.

They haven't mentioned
the terror yet: the shrill and livid joy;
the wilderness that makes messiahs
of many. You make the supper
and the birds, these little black fists,
just hang there like loyal apostles
on the loose, quivering edges
saying nothing, waiting
to be redeemed.

HOW IT WORKS

As the logging truck rounds the corner
its wheels tremble. You know this,
because you are in the oncoming
lane and able to see the rainwater
shiver from its load. The rig
crosses the yellow line into your path;
celestial and righteous, it spreads across
your windshield, an inkwell overturned.
In the time you have, you think you deserve
more than this: a bouncer's arm around your
neck, being dragged from the class,
spanked in a shopping mall, more
than the vertigo, the shrill relief
of such moments, a logging truck barrelling
towards you, blooming from the fingers up,
uncurling from you the split pea
of your heart, the penny left in the till,
the rainbow in the photo that no one
else will see.

SO CLOSE

I walk for an hour
along the gravel breaker
between swells of wheat,
each step sinking deeper
into the aquarium calm:
enormous bodies above me,
armada-white and trailing
the sun, their wake
trickling down the shadow
of my back. Intimacy
is a mute exchange
with the immeasurable,
and returning
       I am drained,
breathless, stumbling up
the wooden steps, tearing
a toenail in the process.
The pain, unanchored,
drifts away.

AIRPORTS

Always, the same bartender
the same pre-flight bookstore
the same blue bay
of fins.
Never a fingerprint,
not a clue as to what
happens. Only
the occasional bottle
of Smirnoff,
lying on the white tiles
of a toilet stall
broken at the mouth.

BALANCE

It's a cappuccino and buttered croissant
at 30,000 feet; filet mignon and a dry merlot
among Antarctic icebergs; a bowl of ice cream
in one hand and the fingers of the other
pressing against a blizzard at 40 below: it's a sweet spot
between comfort and death: as elemental
as the sun on a soap bubble, the creak
of a swing over a river: the daring
to have your bones scattered like silverware
across ocean floors, a comet's tail
among ceiling stars, and you
stretching to the tender verge
of a kite drawn into evening, the string
in your back humming in the abyss.

THE BARE NECESSITIES

We need three mangrove trees,
a bamboo hut,
and a shoreline.

We need a little supply boat
to putter into our bay
of half dreams
every other day.

We need one bald gentleman
with skin like an oiled glove,
one old lady
in a thong,
and one Frenchman
with a young local
companion.

We need the ginger parts
of our bodies
to remain untouched
by the sun, and for the moon
to wash under our huts at night.

We need to go without running water,
to nap anytime we want,
and to bathe in the sea.

We need
to miss things, occasionally
to be the spoiled princess,
the boyish villain.

We need to know
but for our money,
we are hated here
and love
every minute
of our stay.

BURN

The injury
is more on the level
of a paper cut, petty
as a hangnail,
the lingering sting
of a remark made
in bed.

However slight the comment,
I can feel the sunrays bristling
like quills through the mosquito netting,
scattering the geckos
with the hard sweep
of a glare.

I can hear
the snapping of lids,
the growl of a zipper:
the sharp clatter of fingers clutching
at vital little things.

It's amazing
how those rosy fingertips,
that warm glow of breath
can all at once
peel the skin
from an exposed ankle
or strip the covering
from a section of my back:

Your face
through the veil of netting
is bright with sun-block,
your eyes
through the finality of shades
are flowing with tears
that have seared my arm.

You are leaving,
and beyond us
the birds in the trees
are already singing
as fiercely
as the sunburnt dogs
will howl
tonight.

ROAD TO LOVINA

The bus leans into the mountainside,
engine rattling furiously in its casements
as the tin frame around us burrows
into leaves and branches, bounces
across a foot-wide river gorge
and catches long webs of waterfall
in its wipers; through the windows
pagodas are whittled away by idle knives,
monkeys squat along the roadside,
wearing the frowns of old men; dogs
and ragged kids, immune to fenders,
dodge the bald tires of motorcyclists
who squeeze through spaces a sheet
of paper couldn't, the windshield
scrapes against a deep bend in the road
and as we crest into sun, the ocean
is a shining disk far below, and then
we plummet; the guy from South Korea,
the couple from French Belgium,
all of us hit our phantom brakes
as the driver works the gears
like a mad scientist, and on arriving
his daughter pops her head over
the backrest of the front seat to watch
these strange people struggling
for their bags, while fingers are forcing
business cards and brochures through
the window cracks as the bus door
rattles open.

What's your name?
Where you from?
What's your name?

This backyard of a bus station is alive
and these famished greetings are its breath,
and we lean into it, losing the others
as we burrow through the young women
unfurling factory-made sarongs like long
sad stories, the boatmen calling out from
the finger shadows of palm trees,

Lucky Lady!
The Mona Lisa!
The Spectacular!

the names of their catamarans, and the dark-eyed
children, barefoot, voraciously fluent, clutching
tangles of coconut necklaces in their stone-
sized fists and this and this and this all the way
to the shore where hermit crabs hide their heads
and the coral dies in the shallow wane
of the moon.

　　　　　Now the ocean is a pool of dusk
as we step with the solitary grace of cranes,
look down, and release our faces, lanterns
into the sea.

THE PRE-DAWN

The old women come with sarongs
wrapped around their waists
and around bundles
tied to their hips.
They gather by the fountain
and their talk is the rasp
of branches, their fingers
are the scratch of shadows
as they loosen knots
and lay out rice pastries, coconut shreds, banana leaves;
instant coffee streams from thermoses
into the cellar-coolness, where old men shuffle
so tired
you can almost hear
the wooden groan
as they loosen their knees
and work the sockets of their hips
against stone benches, their sweat
catching dawn's breath
between their shoulder blades. The chill
must be as sweet
as a pocketful of coconut sugar
to the girl skipping through a halo of lights,
as the last handful of shadows
to the young couples,
their limbs' ivy
entwining in the dark
corners of the old women's eyes
whose fingers
are by now coated

with coconut juice
whose laughter is
the broken tin roofs
and wrecked sidewalks
of a city that soon will burn
in the sun's heat.

The main streets rattle
with headlights, they groan
with the tires and pistons
of a cold engine. The fountain
in the park springs to life
and three stone figures
wrapped in white sarongs
become visible, high above the crowds.
Their curled sabres raised skywards,
their granite torsos carved from night clouds,
they call for war. But the pastry sellers
only laugh, knowing well
that the stone figures
and the fire
rising to meet them
are part of the same unfolding:
the old women
have timed it right
again. When the predawn veil lifts
with the sun,
they will have sold as much
sweetness as the city needs.

CALL TO PRAYER

A hammer sliding down a clay rooftop,
an old pair of leather shoes scraping over
road dust: the soft torque of breath,
a throat dry as sand, permeate the far wall
of your room with a voice that needs no echo.

Your tile floors are stung with coolness,
and the cry, whose every word is a passage
blazing a Herculean leap, rises from a dozen
hidden rooms around the city. Your sheets
are a blue shroud and the song travels
from district to district from wall to window;
your sun dawns the shadows of water tanks;
the bed is a sundial turning at the centre
of an old stenograph, words crying out as alien
as whale music scratching on your skull.
A horizon of television aerials and satellite dishes
and the relentless mammal lingers there,
its skin above you, the air its bones, the hammer
strokes the slow fury of one who utters God.

BERINGHARJO MARKET

At the entrance
a hawker is selling plastic coat-hangers
and a vagrant
is pulling himself along the floor
through the tangle of feet
with a short stick
and one leg.

He
holds up a paper cup
     and rattles it
         like a cracked bell
and you
ease around him
into the closet maze
of hanging light bulbs
         strung out
like stars
above the boutiques and
crescent faces
of Muslim girls
         digging through
     the latest assortment of bras
the unfading tongues
of old women
     haggling
over days
of Sembal sauce
and hours
of rice

and you
slip by
into the
dark of an alley
between malls
where a fat
sweating man
      without eyes
      plays a drum to the dreams
      of the Bajec drivers
      lying
in their carriages
      stringing galaxies in their sleep
and you
drift
into the rear market
where farm women
wrapped in sarongs
sit on linoleum tiles
before banana hands
      and bowls of rice and
young men
crouch in doorways
to abandoned rooms
novelty key-chain name tags
at their feet
and eternity
          in their fingers
      and you
wander
into the back streets
where butchers

               hack
raw chicken
and pineapples
to pieces
and the pulpers
                    force
the whites
of coconuts
into the blackened mouths
of meat grinders
                    and a woman
ancient
steps from a wooden shack
and looks around
                    stone-faced,
          a statue in a windstorm.
                    Her
pastel blue village dress
          and white hair
are loosely bound
and it is

here, the paradox:

poverty has chiselled
a goddess, and you
actually want to be noticed
but you
are just
a colourful glimpse,
a spectre in hiking boots
and the people here

owe you nothing
for your amazement
but a "hello mistah."

The ancient woman
doesn't even see you
as she spits
a needle point
of phlegm
into the ground
and disappears
into the shelter of her shack.

LET THERE BE NO CARELESSNESS

From an imperial notice on the door
of the Temple of Heaven, Beijing

Purified by three days of fasting
the Son of Heaven makes his way
through the streets. The commoners
and peasants have bolted their windows,
gathered in the dark, their faces
glowing against the clicking hearts
of their wood stoves.
It's the eve of Winter Solstice
when the Emperor turns
past their doors again, famished
as a sharpening stone, cruel
as a moon wheel, and to those
who dare peek, just as beautiful.

A perfect circle, bone white, is Heaven.
The room where it touches Earth
is built without nails, bears no weight.
In its Vault, the Son of Heaven bargains
with The Ruler of the Universe for Him to melt
the silent paradise, summon the anguish
of black soil, the roar of sun-fed fields.
A bargain is reached, the Emperor
retires to The Hall of Prayer of Good Harvest
to meditate upon the light's edge
in the doorway, to wait for the exact
moment to fulfil his oath
and open the promised animal throats
upon the Throne of Heaven.

Sunrise. An impatient caterpillar
has almost reached the Golden Ball
at the Hall's apex when The Ruler catches him
and incinerates the temple with lightning.

For the transgression of the larvae
thirty-two court dignitaries are sentenced
to death. Upon learning of his fate
one of them utters a shrill laugh: the idea
of being both the host and offering at a sacrifice.
The humour of it cut short by the eyes
of his fellow courtiers: blood-still, tranquil
as paradise: a cold room silent but for the distant
clicking of all the hungry little fires in the realm.

EVERYBODY WANTS A DOLPHIN

Yoyo stands high
against his little mast
making ready
on his 60,000-Rupee guarantee;
the other boats,
latecomers,
are making their way towards
us, the *Lucky Lady*
the *46B*
the *28A*
The Fortuna.
Aboard,
young couples with North Face shells and video cameras,
old men with safari hats and foot-long zoom lenses.
Quickly now, Yoyo,
a family of five on *The Fantastic*
is gaining! A fingernail
of light
is peeking over the horizon
and everyone is looking now,
everyone is straining their necks
like us.
Someone whistles.
Fingers point. There!
And *Friends For Ever* cuts loose from the pack.
Move! Move!
Like amoebas spinning in a petri dish
we multiply:
The Beautiful
The Bullet
The Raphael.

The sun
is a blazing disk
in the east
and Yoyo points:
There! There!
Good, Yoyo, good!
We see them:
little blue shiny things
coiling one over the other like florist ribbons.
We are careful
to suppress our excitement lest the others see,
but then all the dolphins come,
a whole school or herd or pride of them
breaking the surface next to us
with little gasps
like children waking from summer dreams.
We are all circling now
like bubbles in a saucer
and dolphins, dolphins everywhere!
Little grey slippery things
sliding in and out
of the water and all
the engines cut
at once.
There is
not a sound
but the breaths of children's dreams,
our dreams,
my dreams,
and the light
is all around. We almost
collide with *The Fortuna*,
Lucky Lady locks pontoons
with *The Spectacular*
as we all crowd in
hoping,

praying
for one of those little dolphins,
one of those little slippery things
to stick its little snout
out of the water
and squeak
just a few lines
only to me,
so that everyone here,
the Taiwanese law students,
the Austrian accountants,
the Indonesian Boatmen
will know
that I am special,
that I was that child
on the Marineland commercial
shaking hands with the world's most
favourite animal.
Yoyo
is making kissing noises,
the dolphins are slipping
in and out on the breaths
of my dreams,
a woman on *The Fortuna*
cries out in song:
for this is my moment.
Let the others keep their photos of waves and grey blurs!
Everybody in the world wants a dolphin
and today
I'm gonna get one!

Acknowledgements

I'd like to thank everyone at Quattro Books for making this book possible. A special thanks in particular to Luciano Iacobelli, whose continual loyal support and encouragement in recent years has been nothing short of invaluable.

I'd like to thank my family, my mother, Harriet, especially, for her life-long encouragement.

Thank you to Phlip Arima and Jacob Scheier for your guidance and advice.

Thank you also to Valentino Assenza, Jason "Ocean" Dennie, Andréa Jarmai, David Newel, Dawna Rae Hicks, and Paisley Rae.

Thank you to all the literary publications and online journals that have published my poetry.

And thanks finally to my wife, Lisa Keophila, for being my rock.